For dear

PASSION IS EVERYWHERE APPROPRIATE

Caroline Griffin

It's true.

With very much love,

Clem /xx

14/2/99

Published in 1989 by Onlywomen Press, Ltd.,
Radical Feminist and Lesbian Publishers,
38 Mount Pleasant, London WC1X 0AP

Copyright © Caroline Griffin 1989.

All rights reserved. No part of this book may be
reproduced in any form or by any means without the
written permission of Onlywomen Press, Limited.

Cover Illustration © Penny Casdagli.

Cover photo © Sandra Hopley.

Printed and bound in Denmark by Norhaven.
Typeset by Columns, Reading, Berkshire, UK.

British Library Cataloguing in Publication Data
Griffin, Caroline, 1950–
  Passion is everywhere appropriate.
  I. Title
  823'.914

  ISBN 0–906500–34–6

For Penny

CONTENTS

The geranium has beaten out its heart	7
Last December	8
Strawberries in the battle-lines	10
'Don't show your feelings on your face'	11
Elizabeth	13
For Judith: I–V	15
I do not lack the idea of loving	19
I have seen your sweat streaming	21
Call this a life lived backwards	22
Liz	25
Last days are like this	27
If my life could be simple	28
We are pressed so close	30
Night. Two women in bed	32
The woman as a phoenix	34
Changes of time and place	35
Wild mothering	36
She suspects the day of greyness	37
Sorry	38
I have wanted to be an angel	39
Waterlow Park	41
Your warm body speaks to me	42
Late January	44
The river	46
Today is full of rain and wind	47
The poem as the shrine	49
The sound of the wave	51
Late morning Sunday	53
Wanting to take it by the scruff of the neck	55
The warning voices of blackbirds	57
All day I am dreaming a forest	58
Pain after all says nothing much	59
Maybe our souls do mingle	60
Making something for my mother	62

The geranium has beaten out its heart

The geranium has beaten out its heart
before the night. Still you are writing.
An apple-tree is furiously identified —
electric light of the insomniac over the wall.
Electric green. The darkness regains.
Past your door   the arterial snake
harsh tail   bright mouth   bites
into the city.

There is no time to wait all day
beside a still pool for miraculous waters
to move. In the corner of your eye
you suspect others of being healed
white garments swirling the high
dignity of ecstasy dripping from the pool.
A lizard could watch more easily.

You are still writing. The inward
pressing of feet in a new landscape.
Who suspects such walking in the
solitary light of this old house
windows open   the moths vanished?

You keep on   with no sun intent
upon your neck   as your forearm
wipes the sweat from the marble steps
you lie on. The water is still cool
as melons, all this contained
in your strong and solitary hands now
waiting for nothing   making your own
miraculous shout.

1988

Last December

Last December   bitter cold   spitting rain
we stood beside a sea coming in
brown thunderous froth & grit.
I was barely able to pick up stones the
fierce wind & spray snatching my breath
and me wanting this. Then

back to London & the damp streets
the Carol Concert. We are lesbians
our clothes   two women together.
I had come here to remember myself
how I'd sung and to see again my music teacher.

You walk onto the stage heavy in sequins
sing the plain line alone
'Hodie Christus Natus Est'. The girls reply
enclosing me   my past streaming
'Hodie Salvator Apparuit'.

But their passion is allowed only as lips moving
lungs breathed   heads straining forward.
The rest must be still & in uniform
bodies awkward & graceful as mine
forget my hands   my tie tucked in
keep my body still.

And it was all laid out for us –
displayed –
the men could lean forward
and catch those notes.
The girls themselves would call it music
putting aside what they know
the awkwardness of growing
and their particular pain.

This was the power of love
expressed in the wrong words,
the power of women together
exposed but not acknowledged,
this was the loving of women
who need to touch –

So many years to learn
we are not sinful people
and passion is everywhere appropriate.

They sing about the boy to come
and he who came to save us
their intent faces reach out
for correctness in their passion.

And I saw me alright –
she stood on one side   she on the other
and you in front
who pulled my heart into my mouth
and told me something was important.

We had the sound and not the words –
not our words. So many years
to feel my heart inside my chest
and trust its movement.

Tell them no one saves us
Tell them the power of women.

1984

Strawberries in the battle-lines

No strawberries in the battle-lines maybe?
I flex the muscles in my head.
Life is too hard at times.
I shout at sleep to take me over.
And it won't – a red-hot battery I am,
Burning up. Sometimes I shout
To keep myself awake.

We are a mass of situation when we meet,
Knotted, fleshy cords, brain tendrils, matted.
How would I choose to see you, or me?
Love's a jangling bell –
Silence maybe.
Eating, music, my lips feeling
Your lips warm,
Our shapes together giving up on words,
Giving up on loss –
Inappropriate red, strawberries, inappropriate mud.

1978

'Don't show your feelings on your face'

'Don't show your feelings on your face' —
I was so grown up I knew you had to love the people
 who let you down.
As they argued I used to go under the stairs
'God, make them stop please'
I was trying to plug up a hole   no tears would come
 out.

I was in the middle, in it, part of them so
desperate to get away exhilarated by rain
and running and you my music teacher —
and not knowing it all, not naming it,
having opinions having always the last word
and not knowing, but knowing
I mustn't cry too much when she left —
the others all cried anyway.
I did only care how I looked for my piano lesson
but not knowing and embarrassed when my mother
 told me.

The moon started catching me on my way home
late and I was lonely   baby-sitting   capable
lonely   but I didn't know it   and I could always
 manage
being good with children. I spoke well in public
but I couldn't tell anyone and suddenly couldn't bear
concerts, sitting sweating, digging my nails in.
I enjoyed kissing him tilting my boater up against the
 wall
and we got on well — 'he isn't just a friend you know' —
maybe it was this contact pushed me closer to saying
'I feel I'm going to die,' which kept coming up and
 coming up.
(Before this, sitting in bed sweating, 'eternity' I said

seeing the planet spinning infinitely without me and
  then
no planet — watching my face to bring me back to now
with foolishness, my foolish face).

'I feel I'm going to die,' I said and I walked out of
  class.
I was doing it to get attention. I was —
Am I just doing this to get attention?
Bright girl, boyfriend, patch her up and push her back.
She thinks too much.

I wonder, psychiatrist, if my grief spelt lesbian to you.
I know you lacked all respect.
Teachers have to move   I knew that
And everyone else cried, it wasn't just me.
You knew I was mourning   I had no opportunity
People let you down and you still love them.

I know I was pushed back
subterranean troubled finding the cracks in me
making the moon run
and the music hold me sacrificial.

This was not my only letting down
and it wasn't by her.
You passed my grief off too cheap
and I didn't know and knew it all —
there was a stream pushed further down
I'm looking at it now.

1982

Elizabeth

Elizabeth — this formality
marks the difference between now & then,
Lizzie — I want to say
we convent schoolgirls were heroic lovers,
unsupported explorers.
What we did put us outside the world we knew
and for a time we held together.

I wanted your certainty
kneeling with you in the church by the river
then watching the floods.
A precise vision I had
the boat slicing through water
wanting to see how it curled   how it
washed the bank
and spread over the pathways.

Remember the world we stepped out of —
the porcelain madonnas   the virtues of silence
men in suits   flickering electric signs —
the boy I kissed on the river-bank
his hand cupping my breast
his leg taut & nervous against mine.
Boys did this & I gave you a warning
trying to say what the world had taught me.

You climb into bed with me
it is impossible to believe   we touch each other
turning away from the world inside me
not that
we were tender   engrossed   but straitened
so straitened   by silence
the narrow bed   your sleeping sister.
We suffered a passion of reaching out

so cramped we bruised each other.
And in the morning the shock
seeing the marks of how we felt
the bruises on our breasts –
we needed wider times.

Remember what they did to us?
Those who were masked –
the teacher walking by who watched us kissing.
The nun whose mask slipped
gripping the table   rising with anger
she asked you what we did –
and searched my poems to find out.

The others used no words.
They did not speak, just sideways sarcasm
and fear. Your phone-call jerked my father's mocking
'Don't forget to say you love her.'

Did they know more than we did?

Going on for a year
no one took care of us
there were no celebrations.
We were lovers, climbers
held by nothing but our feelings.
We searched for clarity & comfort
and they shook us, shook us badly.

A rope trails still between us
reach out   grasp it   angry –
see what we had & what was taken from us?
Refuse to let it go.

1984

For Judith: I–V

I

Sometimes moving in my sleep I touch you half-awake,
and warm, you turn in gentle motion, take my hand,
or hold me in a touch so light it lasts through sleep.

These half-remembered wakings – as though
lying in grass I find the sun still hot
and turn to dream of islands where the sun will
   always shine,
or nudged by waves that roll beneath my back,
I hear the cries of people on the beach
then feel the sea return.

I want to wrap you round me like a shawl,
and ease through dreams and spin out sleep
so fine and strong we never come undone.

II

The child bangs the drum.
He is your sister's child and
A rehearsal for your child.

In stuffy pubs, cold streets and wrinkled sheets
I've pressed this thought-child to me.
I've seen it born and you
Changed and secretive, consumed
With love perhaps or
Some justification for your diminished self.

A child can be no better one I suppose
To eat the discontent you live in
And grow sturdy. (Never fat.
Your sister's child eats fruit, not sweets.)

It makes me cry
To be so lacking all that world
Of tired mother-hood, penances
Of wakeful nights and always
To feed, to clean, to touch –
A vision clearer, old, will mark your effort.

A call so clearly just must be ignored.
I know if I don't eat I'll starve
And then my cry is bread.
What are you hungry for?
The easy vision?
The inevitable result?

I have no answer to that pure cry,
You're not my mother. But
I want my cries to be unreasonable,
Demanding cries. Older
How to answer them is difficult,
But no less urgent.

III

You've chosen to stay where you are
and that's not with me.
I have no choice but to be sad
because I feel it, no choice
but to be lonely that you've gone.
The psychotherapist says
satisfaction should be rooted more organically.
A plant can grow in water can't it?
But I'm sick of water.

That choice brings you contentment,
end of struggles you say.
I tell myself the implications
like blows on the face. Yet later
your arms are round me like a victor's wreath.
I rattle loosely by your side,
rolling away from your decision,
and you turn to me touch my arm.
Are we starting again?
Considerations of pride hold me apart,
ward off your hands as insults.

Perhaps until I end this needing you
a minimal connection cannot hurt.
The change is to define a necessary growth
as one away from you.
But in bed
I swerve to meet your danger.

IV

I know all words are lies,
That truth's a word and
Words are many-sided,
So why repeat a grief
Until it's fixed into a monument?

Perhaps to beat the time that
Tells me you have gone,
Knowing you'll stand beside this page
And never talk of truth. Perhaps
I write to watch the truth
Measured indifference.

V

So the light comes on again.
You are at the door and I
Push from my chair to go to you.

You are waiting, I see now
to be let out of
wherever I am and
whoever these people are.

Your hands are light and dry.
You wait quite patient as I take them
and return them.

1977

I do not lack the idea of loving

I do not lack the idea of loving,
that person I want to be, given some air.
I have walked under the stars with you
and felt like flying   but

here is an old feeling –
getting close to someone
is a possible risk of my safety.
I can't fly. I can scarely own taking more time
to feel your arms around me longer.

If I could start again, now
asserting my right to be loved
a child in this body rightfully here –

I would not thank you for holding me
I would give up   thanks
such gratitude burns   what have I done
to feel grateful for touching
I would give up   absolution

my anger will burn it away.

Without this to start from
the child   the green space
the rest is nothing just
a struggle to be in your imagination
somewhere else in mine.

I feel so heavy,
and speak of these things
as though someone would disagree.

I need to lie   let the quiet build up
my hands open to space
my body flat   be with me
the quiet builds up   I can breathe deeply
feel a stream inside me trickling
I am   and sometimes you are there too.

1984

I have seen your sweat streaming

I have seen your sweat   streaming in the cold of my
    room
your body diving into your own
slippery wet   heart beating fast.
What impelled you I didn't know
what pushed this dive into nowhere   somewhere
the arched neck (yours) straining to retain
some sense of   somewhere else.

You said it was me you felt
but I was lonely and all this perplexed you
tender or pulled out of forgetfulness
by my silence   my too solid imagining
the beating of black plastic in the rain
my decision to leave you to it.

                                                1984

Call this a life lived backwards

(I)   Call this a life lived backwards
this woman   I   am thirty three
still inside my mother
she frowns as I reach out
for anything.
She doesn't want me to go.
Will someone else hold her hand?
She is too young to have children
she is too young to be left alone
but it's choking me –
layers of mothers   have they swallowed each other?
It's too hot.
I would push out but she frowns too much
and her knuckles are tight.

(II)   Divide 'I want' by 'I can'
    there's a lot of wanting left over
top-heavy   foolish   my legs can't carry this
    burden down the street.
Here is a label –
    I am agoraphobic
    and it's so hot
will no one hold my mother's hand ?

and now two stones –
    'I am afraid to travel'
    'I am afraid to be on my own' –
these are cold stones
    use has rubbed off shame and anger.
I could not say this once.
Now I can provide a commentary
    it is a kind of splitting.

This is a life lived backwards —
    to want and then to ask
'what is possible'   this is division
    how can I love myself?
Wanting does not evaporate
    it goes on burning.
I try to kick it into shape
    kick it to understand.
This is myself I talk about.

Yes   I have felt
    a silence round my wanting
    a pause
the bruised mass speaks slowly
    it is too hard to keep on.
This is no way to live.

(III)   Agoraphobia — I have shown consideration
for so long. I am polite —
    oh please don't leave me
politeness hides the smell of fear —
and patient   infinitely patient
it is a long indrawn breath.
I want it all back now.

(IV)   While this poem burns
my body stretches out.
I do not know the name of the sea
I do not try to know it.
I do not pass the waves through my hands
    hunting   what is this
I do not turn from my great strength
    to claw at this water
I do not ask if the sea is reliable.

I can rest on mysteries
my body stretches out upon them
the intense coiling inside me
listens   is here now.
You know some of my loving
in this there is a heavy turning strength.
While the poem burns remember
I am the same woman.

                                                  1984

Liz

You smooth things down, so
So,
Stroke them to stay as they are put –
                                        the children
                                        a sofa-cover
                                        my hand,
to be comfortable.
What does this mean?

That you can move maybe?
Glance into talk,
dive, but
      the children –
you pull out, dripping,
flick thoughts like ash.

Talk tugs hard.
You watch the shape of people
puttings things together,
you watch the strands –
how they do it.

Your hands give out enough,
but warm,
not given out like a star-fish,
brittle with exhaustion.

At night you dive into yourself
the darkness outside   you in a chair
the kitchen quiet   sleeping people
the garden   too dark to see,
your tiredness rolled up to lean against –
I imagine you, thinking.

It's so hard to cry,
You watch your hands moving
smoothing, to press down and feel.
This unending need for comfort.
Wanting change.
Wanting more change.

1978

Last days are like this

Last days are like this —
on a platform
mouthing messages through glass,
and nothing left to do,
we fumble awkward presents
and wish the train would leave.

Or it's a shipwreck, shouting
quick farewells, the clutch of hands.
Mid-air, the glancing faces check provisions
and are lowered from the side.

Last days are like this —
in Yates's, 'Forever Blowing Bubbles'
plays the Trio, dreaming the Titanic;
watching life-boats cast away,
the pianist sips port to sweeten grief.

Well, we paused before we turned.
And whether in weakness, or simply
marking that something happened
grasped a moment out of movement —
I don't know.
'Daisy, Daisy,' sways the Trio,
knowing ice-bergs are exotic.
Sometimes the actual comes warmer than that.

1973

If my life could be simple

If my life could be simple
a brush stroke on a page
you would be there.
And in this shape I make with my hands
you would see a life moving.

river   I want you to touch me
mountain   we hold this space between us
fiercely   mountain   we push against
our hands, our bodies   hold the choice, the space –
ocean   you move on top of me   ocean
your mouth   your tongue presses
choosing again and again   river
I want you to touch me.

Each touch says
        this is how our lives have been
        and this is how we could be.
Each touch makes a life
        more vivid and more possible.
'We are more than we know.'
'There is no such thing as coincidence.'

I bend to kiss your neck   tender says the kiss
tenderness   your powerful shoulders move
reaching towards my breast   you place
my nipple in your mouth   around you
there is all that I can be of mother
here at the edge of you
holding   respectful
You can call this love or work.

Our bodies move   our hands touch
We are more than we know
and meaning rises to meet this touching
creates a new land to walk on
solid surprise at the bend of a river.

I speak of land   but this is creation
how we become more. Our passion breathes
the child in us, not just the past accepted
but the life in us   as vital as
            the kicking baby
            in the amniotic sac —
how can we touch without
            a raging to create
            more space, more life
or knowing that
            tomorrow I can go back
            and trace my footprints?

I want to use all this
gather it up with energy
like a traveller beginning —
knowing the many shrines I've made
to silence fear with beauty.

The passion in my stride contains this fear.
This ground-swell breathing
is what I have despised   it is myself.

I want now to straddle the lashed boards
straining on the waves.
This is not the best I can do
the best is a line of effort
the edge of the waves where the rubble collects —
This is how I move
with you   with myself   to
remember learn and invent.

1984

We are pressed so close

(I)   We are pressed so close
my head is earth   our lips are earth
Oh speak to me only with your breasts
and feel the intimate mud and rubble
of our bodies turning in the stuck boundaries
of this bed   we have talked too much
and now must hunt through eye-sockets –
contact through bone –
whether the light is there.

'There has to be something' –
I clutch at you   there has to be something
which outlasts some rub of the everyday.
And then I push away your hand
make you a woman of straw because
I have more things to say. Oh please
alter my argument.

(II)   Pale light behind the linen blinds
I clamber from my dreams
your chair   your desk
cradle your warm and tender body –
early morning touches.

At last the fire is held
the coals breathe   pale wood flickers.
Each flame needs feeding I think
building intricacies of sticks
cut small enough for this place.
And there have been decisions
where to put our clothes   our books,
making this a home.

Or together on a coach
your head in my lap
on the naughty kids' back seat –
against the engine's hum   the bucking wheels
I sing lullabies and stroke your hair
through country we don't notice.
This is our home together.

(III)   Do not adjust the shape of the fire too much.
Yet I presume to know where the logs fit
where the flames lick.
When the fire falls   watch out
hot coals and scorched wood
tumble from the grate –
and both of us have said out dreams before
with all the naked hope of now
and some regret is part of what we bring
some part of why I forget to love.

(IV)   Pale light into my dreams.
Your warm and loving body
senses mine   sees my thoughts –
it seems trust is your interest
to go on putting your hand next to mine
to hold the same thread
in the labyrinthine home we move through.

'If our lives are not like our dreams
then what's the point of living?'

1985

Night. Two women in bed

The sea is so cold it pulls and
    turns at the edge of the floor
and I struggle to hold out against
    its hand which sweeps across
and leaves me awake and fearful again.

We have burnt incense and candles
    but now the wind blows crystals
down the brown road. Could we set off
    across the glittering black ice
our scarves sieving the air for warmth?
    Would the other place be any different?
Here you try to tease me alive
    but there are waves
tearing up the room   it's no good
    an opening I can't close
waves are licking the lips of my mouth
    I keep words there and can recite
begin to move   almost   the imperceptible
    gestures of one trying politely
to hold down the sea.
    Sleep wants to make you still
you're leaving me   I can't say
    can't let go   your shelves are
a tension of wood and wire.
    'You act as though I'm not here'
you say   and in that fire of affronting
    I'm saved, pitched by anger
towards you.

Can you account for how we lay
    after our anger and tears
fixed in the forms of sleep yet
    alert to a deep turning
almost exhausted   almost not wanted
    not the skirl of the tide-race —
waiting the waves' motion with
    our heads pressed to the pillow

Our heads pressed to the pillow
    until you turned
and took my mouth
    a shock so fierce and wanted
lick my lips
    I want to feel you catch me
let my mouth be blurred and loose
    open   to our arched and turning
bodies   crying out
    touches which I feel as pain
pain in us   the clarity of fire
    and you touch me deeply
again and again.

                                                    1985

The woman as a phoenix ...

Well her ribs are sometimes taut
like a bird's   when there is pain
womens' hands search beneath her shoulder blades
there may be wings   she is ready for flight often but
her medium is earth   not air
she may lie on it
with the pain of all she has not said
beating in her ribs

there is fierce heat   she walks
to find water   her feet on cold stone
and shaking she tries to let the heat
pass through to earth   regret
the self alone in such a situation.

there is fierce holding
to the place   the body   the night
she has smoothed her body from crown to toe
her pubic hair warm – a lying damp
between bone hips the brown line from
navel to hair   this body that she will die with

there is no holy fire to make her anew
'again and again' is a heavy weight and she
sometimes forgets there is not one of her
her spiritual crises are often in the night
beside the washbasin   give her respect
it makes a fragile bridge between the night
and day   she will grip tightly just as
long as it takes.

1985

Changes of time and place

Tomorrow is hungry,
Tomorrow fills itself with my concerns.
Last week I fed on darkness in my head
Until tomorrow ate it
And was empty.

Now work is hard but
Hooks into my cheek and picks me up,
And makes me feel the iron in my blood.

I would prefer tomorrows
Without hooks or hunger.

1978

Wild mothering

Strong thighs astride my chest
your body presses wet against me
draws up passion as we meet and
yes   your hands press down my palms

I watch you seek me out
this powerful mother who
licks her child with passionate tongue
whose urgent fingers
                    touch my lips
                    open my mouth
                    hold your breast to me –
this is the freedom of wild mothering
to choose
to reach for a hand we don't let fall.

And we can hold together in a circle
our bodies cradle an energy
which spills in sweat in breath in cries
and choose to see our faces as we flow.

                                                            1984

She suspects the day of greyness

She suspects the day of greyness
this is not commonplace but
frequent   gets up
holds the ordinary day in her heart
for a moment – it leaps and kicks
this is familiar not ordinary
she puts the day down
picks herself up
tries to breathe
this is habitual but hard
breathes out   suspects the day
of holding up her life
longs to be held
holds tight to her books and her letters
repeats her name
suspects her bag of weighing more than she does
relies on it
her ordinary life
hopes her heart will on on beating
hopes her life will not mind her questions.

1985

Sorry

Can I give you anything?
Do you need anything?
Can I buy you a drink?
Can I try on your glasses?
What can you see?
Shall I light your cigarette?
Shall I smoke your cigarette?
Shall I tell you a joke?
Shall I make you laugh?
Do you need anything?
Can I sip your drink?
I'm sorry.
Did I knock your foot?
I'm sorry.
Do you want a drink?
Have I asked before?
I'm sorry.
Don't smile at me like that.
Don't lean against me.
Did I knock you?
I'm sorry.
Did you lean against me?
Do you need a match?
Am I flippant?
Are you serious?
Do you want a drink?
Do you need anything?
I'm sorry.

1975

I have wanted to be an angel

Now with these warm hands
and my fierce breath I can say
I've wanted to be an angel. In this
I am against my own body   I feel
the ruin in me   only the dull thud
of flesh on bone   the clumsiness of pain.

Here I see you sleeping under a tree
when you wake and walk further
I may touch the impress in the grass
the marks you have made   noting the difference
the surprise of the turn where my fingers slip.

But we did see each other   we do touch
the heavy press of your weight brings me
to my shape — again and again
we share the weight of our warm bodies
and this is a choice about pain.

I have wanted to be an angel   to leave
and return with infinite grace
wanting only the right touches —
as though we could live without history.

My fierce breath says sometimes
it is like this – bodged attempts,
trying to make, trying to make things up
the great body shuddering – tears
of water or fire clearing a way
through dust through habit
and the voice   the blurt   which leaps out
hardly recognised
jumping ahead into rough country
well   halt then for a while
and feel that wet heaviness rolling through.

We are angels   women   heavy like lumber
and sometimes I lie my face to the wet earth
and rest on it.

1984

Waterlow Park

I can smell the earth   brown   slippery leaves
you hold my hand firmly   fine rain
branches   at this distance   soft   an open flower
December   and rose-hips on the same tree.

I watch your eyes follow the circle of a bird
as it slowly turns and settles where
we could not predict. So we try
to turn towards what we want –

but you are not here now to hold my hand
I understand little   how the Park
goes on existing   that you're sad and I
keep interrupting.

'Thought and memory are mechanical processes
which take us away from the present.'
What must I embrace to know simplicity
when I see it?

We crossed the Thames   a river so extraordinary
still pulled by tides   still reaching
from this straitened place towards the sea.
You are in your house   I in mine
I want your hand.
What times will allow us to live in them
nor is it time's fault –
our striving felt so long ago
I wonder how we ever sense a course
that fits us, links us to a mouth
spilling properly into the sea.

1984

Your warm body speaks to me

Your warm body speaks to me.
We stretch out   speaking with bones.
Still wanting to hold
but not possess   to touch
but not press in.

Outside my room there was your house
a castle of nests drenched by the moon.
When I arrive there will be
a great fire   a circle of lights
and then the walk to the roof
the bright city and a morning of
birds and branches.

Light falls into this house –
the beam of imagination and your hand
draws me. Early journeys –
the bus stepped onto like a burning chariot,
trusting a place to exist
trusting ourselves to exist outside.
And in the winter nights
dreaming of somewhere else
to avoid the traffic   the late bus
the stuck face of everyday life.

You have made so many journeys.
No dreams should obliterate the facts of effort
how you travelled in a blizzard
trains rubbed out   the city stopped
you arriving frail and spent.
Remember the warm evenings
the bus which holds us home
when I listen for your hand
and no one's foot is tracking us.

We have made so many journeys,
we move to touch and move again –
the idea has not gone cold.
We did not hold it like a trophy
it does not rattle in a drawer
opening   when I think back to a time.
In the worst summer for fifty years
your kitchen is full of sweet-peas, daisies
marjoram, thyme and sage.
No dreams should obliterate the facts of effort.
Did we make the garden?
How hard it is to sit under the bay-tree
without a continuous making
a continuous move to snatch up the space
I see opening.

Ideas   effort   sometimes I spring forward
with the intensity of all I do not know
hoping to meet you again
hoping to go on with it all.

1986

Late January

It is late January.
The logs show white and cold
on the blunt earth.
A heron passed here in early Summer,
the sky was blue
but not pared down by this blade
this Sunday morning.

Half the garden is under ice.
I touch the honey-suckle.
There are signs I can't interpret
not wanting to disturb.

But the logs could be carried in –
justify a life with work
that stays put, threads
which don't unravel overnight.

Stillness. The opportunity to be still.
We say our bodies are like rocks,
the outcrop on a moor,
rained on   burnt.
When I feel you as a hard wet rock
I hear the wind of the moor blowing
as your lips touch my ear.

In such stillness I can wander,
like a day off   like a considered risk,
wandering into a slip of my past
a slip on the ice when I didn't cry.

I cry now.
I burrow into your warm body
which suggests as clearly as your mind
a way back to all the sudden stops
rearing up to catch me.

If in the furrow of a gutter
I met a latent hand which
pulled me down   and
if I fell again
wandering from the marker-stone
of my own weight   this time
I came up into your warm arms.

Before the logs are stored
before any cause or reasonable labour
there must be a place to wander
as simple as this morning –

to dream a life without necessity,
or recognising that place to be
as simple as your arms
as a garden
which a heron passes in early Summer,
its flight as random and particular
as noticing.

1986

The river

Through the meshed window of this institution
the ice-cap is melting.
A cawl of snow glistens on the tundra.

I know a cold green river
winding through fields   a view
beyond   unknown
grass blades held in ice
silence as a swan passes.

We talk in light voices of our burdens.
They weigh us down.

The silence of this river
is thirsty in my throat.
I grip the spare branches
the rough bark which cuts through.

You are my comrade.
In the middle of the tundra
we meet in rags
our lashes crusted with snow.
We know how hard it is to trudge.

But I have spun round you
with the speed of the ice-dancer's torque,
the arc of a hack-saw,
beginning from balance
and moving into flames.
Release the tatters of labour.
You are thirsty too.
When we forget the river
our holiness vanishes.

1986

Today is full of rain and wind

Today is full of rain and wind
the trees are showing the underside,
branches pushed too far back.
Today the bean-poles sway and I wonder
what holds, what catches,
remember the tight knots of sweet-peas
so light the wind can't tear them,
so light we can't be torn –

What holds, what catches?
The branches are pushed too far back.
Blake saw angels in the trees
I see my father, he is very small
and asking for some reason not to jump.
I give him a reason.

'By the Cross her station keeping
stands the Queen of Sorrows weeping' –
the road runs between Highgate and Golders Green
very straight, trees both sides. I see myself
standing there at risk to earth and sky –

The logs have been stored in a dry place.
They flare up now, efforts
towards an outcome beyond the power of our
   imagining,
visions, as though some being in magnificence
   emerged,
as though a lion roared in a corner of this quiet room –
and I see myself crying on the road
between Highgate Hill and Golders Green
crying out for you,
unable to be alone,
unable to put myself there.

Here is no glory.
I give away my pain. I burn my efforts
which might break through
into myself being alone.

I see angels everyday
they run off all the time anytime
leaving the everyday to me.
Blake saw angels in the trees.
I see my father, he wants to know why,
and I see a woman weeping in the road –
visions of suffering
towards an outcome beyond the power of my
   imagining.
I cry out for you – trying to hold on –
Is this in the nature of things?
None of us can bear it all the time.

1985

The poem as the shrine*

panic—   a deep attachment to struggle
         breaking out in dark places.
            woods   sweat   and the bark of trees,
               shrines.
panic—   a deep attachment to experiencing fear
         a deep attachment to notice   to see
            flowers   to hunt the shrine   in the
               woods.

panic throbbing and rocking the tree is still
            the air is still
            is this asthma
            the difference between myself and the tree
               is lost
            and all the fine words count for nothing
            compared with this
            bitterness that a walk becomes
            this struggle.
            Flowers have names and
            people stroll.

   I carry an offering   a shriek maybe
   of panic —
   a deep attachment to assertion/testing
   that there is another   out there.
   I offer up this   and find
   the earth is hard and unyielding
   it proves nothing clutching at earth
   dirt on my hands my nails sting
   I am indeed operated on by what I feel.
   My fear eats up the world.

The shrine was put there —
a personal victory
the assertion of meaning
in the calm of survival.
But I can't stand the hammering.
I have stood here long enough.

The squirrel pushing through a fence
jolts me and vibrating on a tree trunk
becomes my fear   the shudder in the tree
a jagged branch strikes me.

Plunge the hands deep
tear out myself?
It is not possible.
There are words wrung out of fear
words I carry in my head until
the symbols of a room and walls allow
some separateness. Then
I can look on and survive.

panic—   a deep attachment
          to experience   fear   breaking out.

*shrines to Pan were often in secret wooded places

1981

The sound of the wave

The sound of the wave is loud enough
to release this cry
'What if we are just stones' –
allowing the rush
the parted waters coming together
the words gasped out in the wake of
the wave pulling down the shore
the glistening backs rolling over and over.
'What if we are just stones,'
meaning equality coherence.

Between the ship and the shore
a weathered plank – my body.
My body is as hard as a fist.
Wait   I am going somewhere
I am holding movement still
and the speed of passion is infinite
hard and flooding   the plank
the spring-board.

I am also a frog.
My thighs kick and push
feeling your spine between my legs.
And light floods in
light floods out.
Is the passion of frogs to leap?

Later the mist was almost rain
tangible   I could wipe it away
and the stronger leaves held up bright pools.
The tulips are in rags.
We did not see them leap
to this state.

The world is not kind
it is full of pain
and this awareness breaks through
with a shout
to annihilate all images —
the unbearable nature of things
is not represented in any diagram —
only sit still long enough to draw one
to observe the possibilities.

We are not still ourselves.
We roll over and over like the unsevered worm
coiling round our hurt
whipping the earth in pain.

Sometimes the clarity of rocks and streams
is not for us   there is heat
the fact of pain
why we might want to break
into   away from   out
why the breaking together
is a unity   like sharing tears
like recognising tatters when we see them.

1986

Late morning Sunday

Late morning Sunday   and even here
we drag the day in like a sticky tail
to which everything accumulates.
The sun is brittle and temporary
and still the trails of the everyday
rasp as we turn
sighing only for our own selves
our own tiredness.

This is the day we move furniture
heavy   slow   pausing to consider.
We pull dead weights up the stairs.
Leaves rot on the lawn hiding
ceaseless and increasing worm activity.
I leave them to it.
The constant air plays into this gap
the hole in the link in the chain of links
which still keeps moving and has no name
unlike the eye of the needle or the hurricane.
It is Sunday afternoon   I am
scared to go into it.

The publican is lonely
his wife has gone to China
her father is dying   my friend's mother is dead
my own mother is dead.
I gave a present to my friend –
'This is from your mother,'
meaning me   a joke   meaning
for a moment I forgot so both of us cried.
Am I not able to use the word anymore?

The everyday roars beside us
a ticker-tape which I have no choice
but to read   the same words I call
a sticky trail when I am lonely
recognising with you
it is the terrain in which we live
and without naming or knowing
in which we drown.

I see my hand flailing
failing to catch the rail
or holding too tight.
I need your hand to read
the way things are
to hear my cry as the bus lurches
and I spray myself with beer
held also for protection
like the man who begs in the underpass.

Sunday afternoon.
Your hair still curls just in front of your ears.
The room was warm
and I saw your body as simple and separate
while you held me.
Even now I have left these facts to the end.

1987

Wanting to take it by the scruff of the neck

Wanting to take it by the scruff of the neck
and shake it   a ruff of hair gathering
and staring into the sharp teeth.

Wanting to pick up something by the scruff of the
   neck
and hurl it   because the dust on the stairs teaches
only patience over and over.

Stepping onto a bright wheel
blazing above the Common
held only by gravity   by the nature of things
and wanting to step off   not wanting to wait
because being born is a circular route
and no-one asked permission.

There was the sea   unfamiliar   distinct
and we rushed into it –
a squandering sea   obliterating plans
against which nothing can stand.
We swam naked   with no resistance
a continuous rocking and tumbling
over our breasts. Later
our skins dried salt in the sun
and the pebbles were warm.
Against the embrace of the waves
which was no embrace
we were then people who knew
the impossibility of swallowing the sea.

We have tried.
'A person can't live on air or postage stamps.'
With what confidence and how often
we have climbed to the top of a hill
holding balloons. They fly undeniable
trailing our secret dreams —
but there are other hills if we choose.
The sea tells us there is real earth.

Let us spit out the mountain   the taste
of gravel in our teeth and the sky
like a blanket   so heavy —
sometimes our minds hold up the world.

How hard the year has been.
The clematis trails a corona about the privet.
Past the window the evening glitters in a seed-head
and continues.

1985

The warning voices of blackbirds

Over these fences
the warning voices of blackbirds
ring like hammers beating out
the cadences of ordinary speech.

Green shades of the eucalyptus
and behind it the poplar.

My jacket I swing round is black
like a cape   a fighting cape
swinging loose stones in the pockets.
The stones resound as weapons.

I have walked under so many arches
under which they carry the dead.

This is the place of holes.
It is so precious. I must belong here.
This is where I come from
and return to.

I see I am a guardian.
There are quarrels over the marker-stones.
The granite chips have been taken
they were green   not like any stones
I've ever seen.

Sail out my cape.
The stones resound as weapons.
The rubble in the earth is a debris
which cannot be cleared and
the noise of a blackbird pulling its worm
is not the only punishment.

1986

All day I am dreaming a forest

All day
I am dreaming a forest.
Leaves and the forks of branches
hold me in a darkness
deeper than the daily tasks
ringing in my head
and in my hands.

How heavily the bee walks
abdomen dipping with each step –
but ours was
no dry wings or
urgent hive.

You dip against me
heavy with light.
Our lips meet
forming that O now
joined and shuddering down.

All day I return to you.
touch the damp hair
back across your forehead,
wanting this damp   this
mortal tenderness
more than any river   essence
we may become
or any other darkness.

1987

Pain after all says nothing much

Pain after all says nothing much –
too busy holding its own shadows
chest tightened like a husk.

But last night
I hold your body and
all the rest falls away.
We are bodies defying funereal sculpture
yet belonging to the earth
and naked and still.

The embrace.
Laurel leaves and ivy growing
round and round the corrugated bark.
Your face is damp with tears
I have pressed your face into –
the rest falls away.

We are under a greenwood tree
for the moment and our lips
are clay but warm   I can't help it
but clay.

Now small embers of the fire
catch and relight,
circles of soot squirm hastily
across the grate.
This is the earth in which
grief is allowed to occur,
embracing in darkness   with no moon
not reaching forwards or back to
anything except holding on
to this mortal state.

1987

Maybe our souls do mingle

Maybe our souls do mingle
when we're together for now
I'm heat and chaos struggling
to name a feeling. Loss.
The word becomes a self
I try to hold through all
the rapid transformations.

But now I am gulping air
a new surprised creature
new to my body to land or sea
a curious amphibian
clutching at any speckled stone.

When did I eat the bitter fruit
which makes this no new world?
Likewise I desire to hide
from anything – the light on my skin
the body's immense need for air
and terrible regularity
until the final monotone.
I see sweat on my hand while
enormous rivers race
and Autumn light burns inescapable
on dead and falling leaves.

Help me.
There is a tree in glorious silence.
I think   if there are angels
this is an angel. Unspeaking:
'O tree, you overtopped the ecstasy
of my bubbling blood, you were
the crown of passion and its bearer.'

Unspeaking. I walk into the familiar world
and rivers turn. It seems
I am not yet out of the Garden of Eden
meaning   for a moment I took my place
justly amongst the grass and found
the whip of fear I do not need
to bring me to my knees.

1989

Making something for my mother

Find driftwood from the garden —
brown damp not salt —
I light a candle. The wood is
broken off and the grain exposed
ridges   the grain of a wave.

The last time I saw my mother
she held my hand as we walked
down the narrow and precarious steps
of a hotel. Her hand was hot.
I think she was nervous.

And what did I say? Nothing.
We hugged in the Ladies Powder Room.
I think we did. Toiled back upstairs.
There were small cakes and a man
at a piano played Chopin —
not as well as my mother.

Her hands were hot and nervous.
I melt wax   tear small pieces of tissue.
I want flakes of gold to anoint her.
The wind howls between corridors
of Himalayan mountains and in the
gasping pain of high altitude
another stone is rolled to the cairn.

Though dead you are still my mother.
Her flag flies above them all
trailing a cry in thin cold air.
May grief not whip a garland to shreds.
The wind can spin out streamers
perfumed with her name   a fine thread
that will go down any valley
we choose to remember or forget –
the spun name encircling Tibetan stones
polished by rain from higher mountains.
On the roof of the world
her name is a blazon.

She powdered her face.
We toiled back upstairs. Now is
wood and clay   paper and candle-light
to melt and burn   score and flame over.
No trumpet can sound her name loud enough.

I write her name in pencil
on tissue-paper. Against a twig
upright in the wood a fragment
of wax secures it   translucent and
I add more flags   prayer-flags
to what is now a tree   a mast.

1989